WELCOME TO THE U.S.A.

SOUTH DAKOTA

Written by Ann Heinrichs   Illustrated by Matt Kania
Content Adviser: Ronette Rumpca, Curator of Interpretation,
Museum of the South Dakota State Historical Society,
Pierre, South Dakota

The Child's World®

J 917.83
Heinrichs

Published in the United States of America by The Child's World®
PO Box 326 • Chanhassen, MN 55317-0326
800-599-READ • www.childsworld.com

Photo Credits
Cover: Photodisc; frontispiece: Melvyn P. Lawes/Papilio/Corbis.

Interior: AP/Wide World Photo: 17 (Charles Bennett), 29 (Rapid City Journal/
Bill Cissell); AP/Wide World Photos/Doug Dreyer: 9, 18; Corbis: 6 (Paul A.
Souders), 10 (Tom Bean), 13 (Jim Richardson), 14 (Robert van der Hilst), 22
(Tim Thompson), 25 (Sean Sexton Collection), 30 (Joseph Sohm/ChromoSohm
Inc.), 33 (Carl & Ann Purcell), 34 (Richard T. Nowitz); Photodisc: 26; Tabor Area
Chamber of Commerce: 21.

Acknowledgments
The Child's World®: Mary Berendes, Publishing Director

Editorial Directions, Inc.: E. Russell Primm, Editorial Director; Katie Marsico, Associate
Editor; Judith Shiffer, Assistant Editor; Matt Messbarger, Editorial Assistant; Susan Hindman,
Copy Editor; Melissa McDaniel, Proofreader; Kevin Cunningham, Peter Garnham, Matt
Messbarger, Olivia Nellums, Chris Simms, Molly Symmonds, Katherine Trickle, Carl
Stephen Wender, Fact Checkers; Tim Griffin/IndexServ, Indexer; Cian Loughlin O'Day,
Photo Researcher and Editor

The Design Lab: Kathleen Petelinsek, Design and Art Production

Library of Congress Cataloging-in-Publication Data
Heinrichs, Ann.
   South Dakota / by Ann Heinrichs ; cartography and illustrations by Matt Kania.
     p. cm. — (Welcome to the U.S.A.)
   Includes index.
   ISBN 1-59296-483-4 (library bound : alk. paper)
   1. South Dakota—Juvenile literature. I. Kania, Matt, ill. II. Title.
F651.3.H455 2006
978.3—dc22   2005016609

**About the Author
Ann Heinrichs**

Ann Heinrichs is the author of more than 100 books for children and young adults. She has also enjoyed successful careers as a children's book editor and an advertising copywriter. Ann grew up in Fort Smith, Arkansas, and lives in Chicago, Illinois.

**About the
Map Illustrator
Matt Kania**

Matt Kania loves maps and, as a kid, dreamed of making them. In school he studied geography and cartography, and today he makes maps for a living. Matt's favorite thing about drawing maps is learning about the places they represent. Many of the maps he has created can be found in books, magazines, videos, Web sites, and public places.

On the cover: **Mount Rushmore features the faces of 4 famous presidents.**
On page one: **Want to go back in time? Visit Deadwood and learn about the Wild West!**

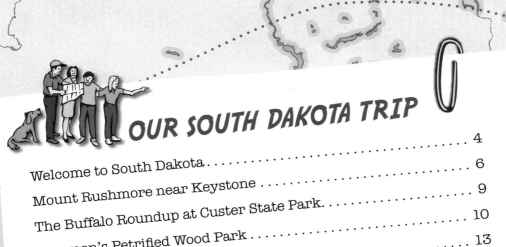

OUR SOUTH DAKOTA TRIP

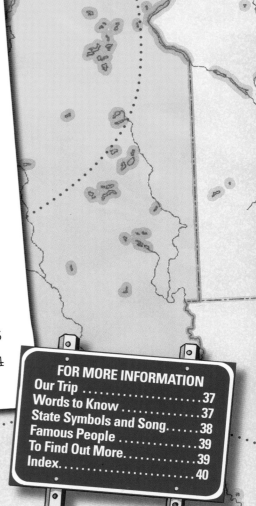

South Dakota's Nickname:
The Mount Rushmore State

Hey—let's take a tour of South Dakota. You'll find it's a great place to explore!

You'll walk the streets of Wild West towns. You'll watch herds of buffalo galloping by. You'll see giant faces carved in mountainsides. You'll visit a palace covered with corn. You'll roam through **prairies** and see **missile** sites. And you'll hang out with real cowboys!

Are you ready for adventure? Then settle in and buckle up. It's time to hit the road!

WELCOME TO SOUTH DAKOTA

As you travel through South Dakota, watch for all the interesting facts along the way.

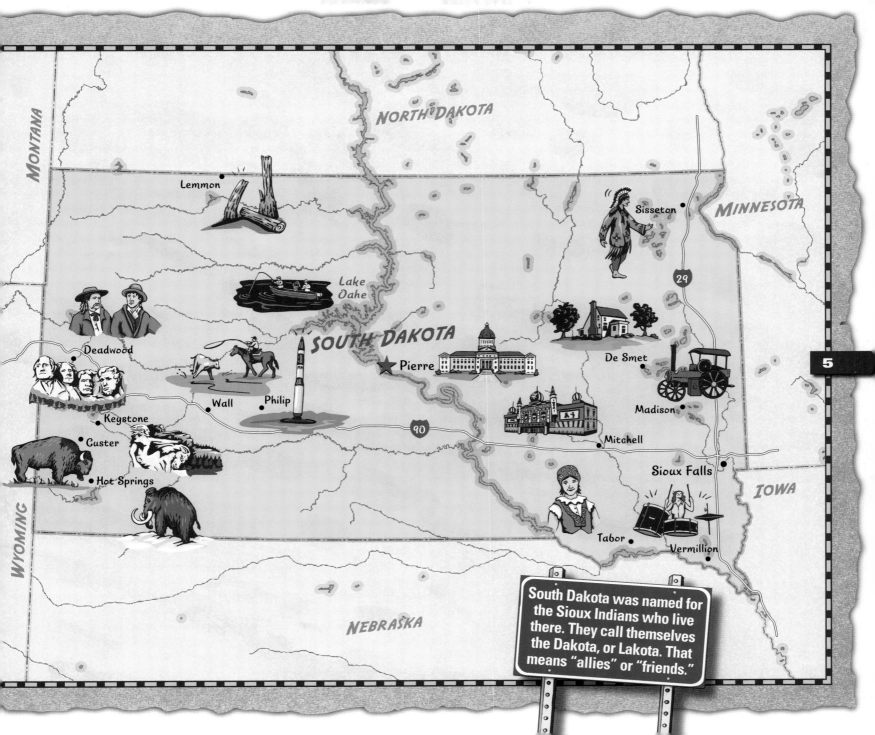

MONTANA

NORTH DAKOTA

MINNESOTA

Lemmon

Sisseton

29

Lake
Oahe

SOUTH DAKOTA

De Smet

Deadwood

★ Pierre

Madison

Keystone

Wall   Philip

Custer

Mitchell

Hot Springs

Sioux Falls

IOWA

Tabor

Vermillion

WYOMING

NEBRASKA

South Dakota was named for
the Sioux Indians who live
there. They call themselves
the Dakota, or Lakota. That
means "allies" or "friends."

5

Mount Rushmore is a reminder of 4 famous presidents.

Mount Rushmore near Keystone

Have you seen these faces before? They're four U.S. presidents. And they're carved right into the mountain. You're visiting Mount Rushmore!

This awesome mountain is in the Black Hills. Among these hills are forests, canyons, and caves. The Badlands are southeast of the Black Hills. This is a dry region with strangely shaped rocks.

The Missouri River is South Dakota's major river. It flows south, then southeast, through the state. To the west are rugged canyons and rolling plains. Eastern South Dakota has rich farmland. It's dotted with many small lakes, too.

Wind Cave National Park is near Pringle. Jewel Cave National Monument is near Custer.

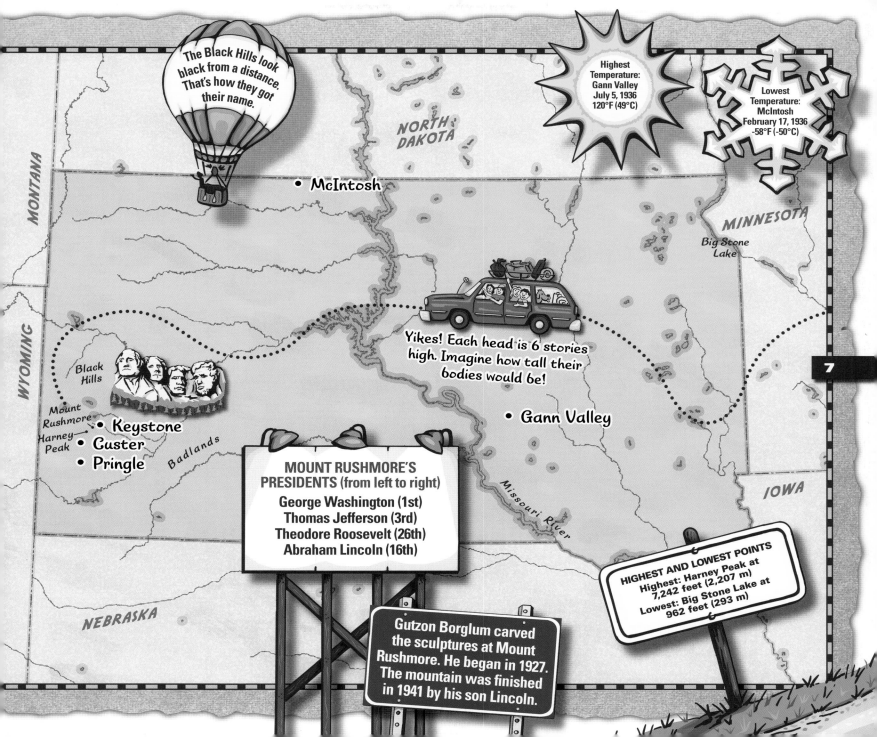

The Black Hills look black from a distance. That's how they got their name.

NORTH DAKOTA

Highest Temperature: Gann Valley July 5, 1936 120°F (49°C)

Lowest Temperature: McIntosh February 17, 1936 -58°F (-50°C)

MONTANA

McIntosh

MINNESOTA

Big Stone Lake

WYOMING

Yikes! Each head is 6 stories high. Imagine how tall their bodies would be!

Black Hills

Mount Rushmore

Harney Peak

Keystone

Custer

Pringle

Badlands

Gann Valley

Missouri River

IOWA

MOUNT RUSHMORE'S PRESIDENTS (from left to right)

George Washington (1st)
Thomas Jefferson (3rd)
Theodore Roosevelt (26th)
Abraham Lincoln (16th)

HIGHEST AND LOWEST POINTS
Highest: Harney Peak at 7,242 feet (2,207 m)
Lowest: Big Stone Lake at 962 feet (293 m)

NEBRASKA

Gutzon Borglum carved the sculptures at Mount Rushmore. He began in 1927. The mountain was finished in 1941 by his son Lincoln.

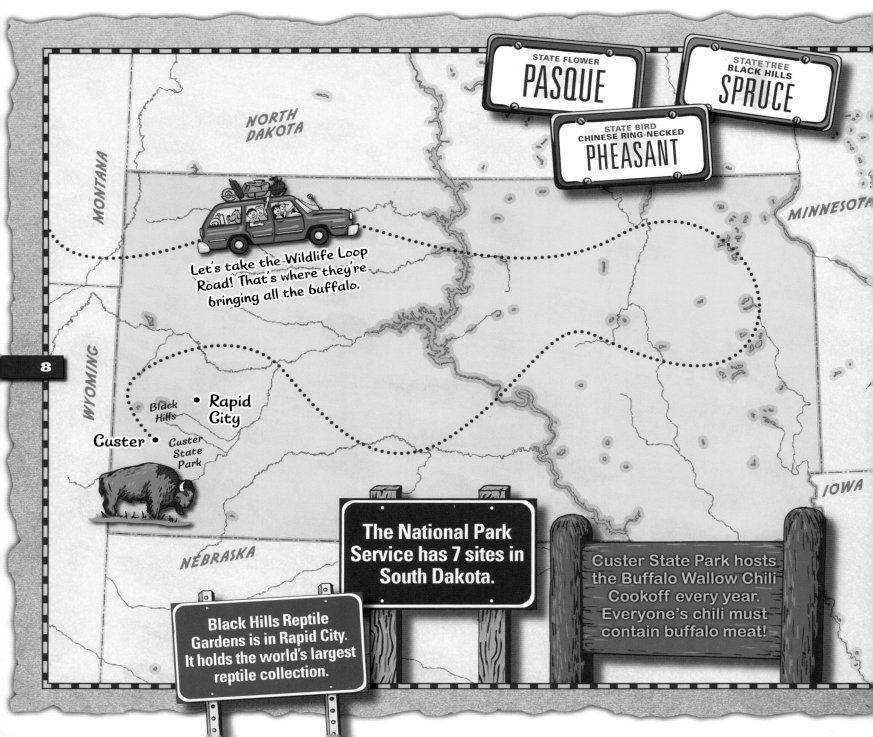

STATE FLOWER
PASQUE

STATE TREE
BLACK HILLS
SPRUCE

STATE BIRD
CHINESE RING-NECKED
PHEASANT

NORTH DAKOTA

MONTANA

MINNESOTA

Let's take the Wildlife Loop Road! That's where they're bringing all the buffalo.

WYOMING

Black Hills

• Rapid City

Custer • • Custer State Park

IOWA

NEBRASKA

The National Park Service has 7 sites in South Dakota.

Custer State Park hosts the Buffalo Wallow Chili Cookoff every year. Everyone's chili must contain buffalo meat!

Black Hills Reptile Gardens is in Rapid City. It holds the world's largest reptile collection.

The Buffalo Roundup at Custer State Park

Cowboys and cowgirls gallop across the plains. They're herding buffalo into **corrals.** It's the Buffalo Roundup at Custer State Park!

About 1,500 buffalo roam through this park. Every year they're rounded up. They get medical care, and some are sold.

This park is near Custer in the Black Hills. Many other animals make their homes here. Some live high in the mountains. You'll see mountain goats and bighorn sheep in this area. On the prairies are deer and pronghorn antelope. Prairie dogs dig tunnels to build their towns. You'll spot elk, coyotes, and wild turkeys, too.

Yeehaw! Move 'em out! Don't miss the Buffalo Roundup at Custer State Park.

Those rocks were trees 50 million years ago!
Check out the Petrified Wood Park.

Lemmon's Petrified Wood Park

Stroll down the winding paths. This is no ordinary park. It has buildings with towers on the corners. And tall, pointy cones. Here and there are weird stumps and logs. You're wandering through the Petrified Wood Park!

Most things in this park are wood. But it's petrified, or turned to stone. The wood once belonged to giant trees. They were alive 50 million years ago!

You'll see stone slabs in the park, too. Look closely, and you'll spot prints of grasses. Those grasses also lived millions of years ago. Could dinosaurs have been nibbling grasses then?

Dinosaurs lived in South Dakota about 150 million to 66 million years ago.

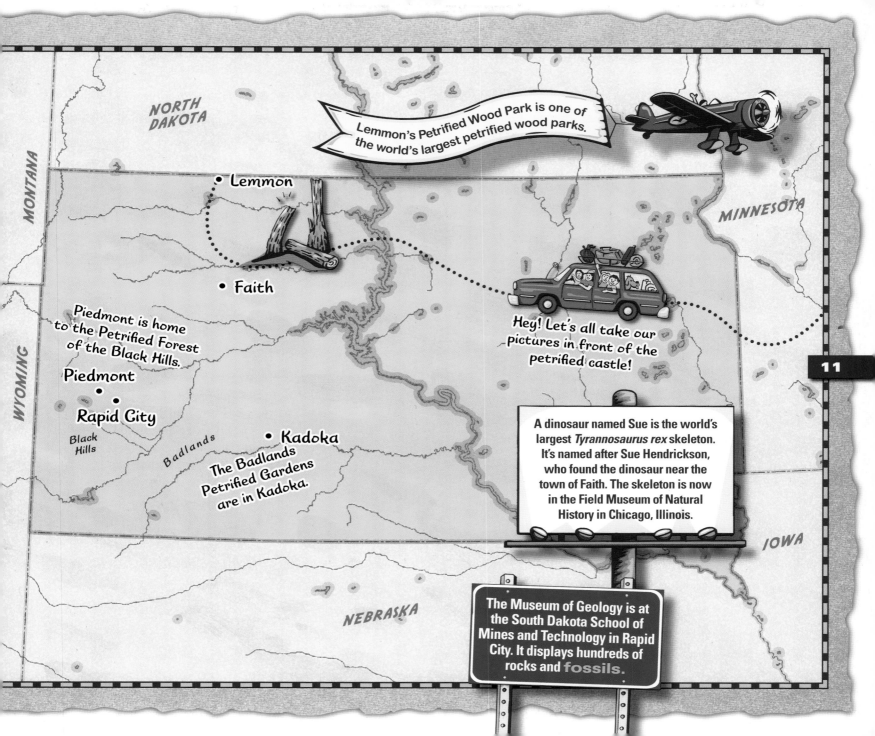

NORTH DAKOTA

MONTANA

MINNESOTA

Lemmon's Petrified Wood Park is one of the world's largest petrified wood parks.

• Lemmon

• Faith

Piedmont is home to the Petrified Forest of the Black Hills.

Piedmont •

• Rapid City

Black Hills

WYOMING

Badlands

• Kadoka

The Badlands Petrified Gardens are in Kadoka.

Hey! Let's all take our pictures in front of the petrified castle!

A dinosaur named Sue is the world's largest *Tyrannosaurus rex* skeleton. It's named after Sue Hendrickson, who found the dinosaur near the town of Faith. The skeleton is now in the Field Museum of Natural History in Chicago, Illinois.

IOWA

NEBRASKA

The Museum of Geology is at the South Dakota School of Mines and Technology in Rapid City. It displays hundreds of rocks and **fossils.**

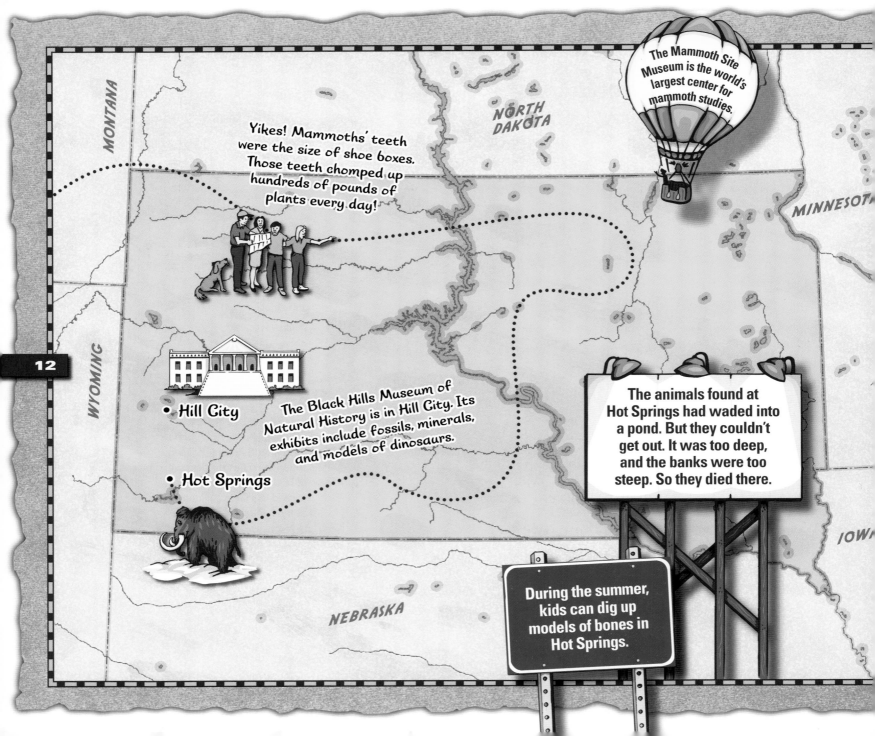

The Mammoth Site Museum is the world's largest center for mammoth studies.

Yikes! Mammoths' teeth were the size of shoe boxes. Those teeth chomped up hundreds of pounds of plants every day!

The Black Hills Museum of Natural History is in Hill City. Its exhibits include fossils, minerals, and models of dinosaurs.

• Hill City

• Hot Springs

The animals found at Hot Springs had waded into a pond. But they couldn't get out. It was too deep, and the banks were too steep. So they died there.

During the summer, kids can dig up models of bones in Hot Springs.

MONTANA

NORTH DAKOTA

MINNESOTA

WYOMING

NEBRASKA

IOWA

Walk through the dig site. Around every corner are big bones. Some are skulls with huge, curved tusks. This is not just a big museum. It's a mammoth museum!

You're visiting the Mammoth Site Museum. It's built right on a scientists' digging place. They discovered lots of mammoth bones here.

Mammoths lived here about 26,000 years ago. These massive, shaggy beasts were related to elephants. We sometimes use the word *mammoth* to mean "gigantic."

Many other animals were found in this spot, too. But mammoths were the most mammoth of them all!

Want to learn about prehistoric animals?
Tour the Mammoth Site Museum!

13

Two kinds of mammoths were found at Hot Springs. They are the Columbian mammoth and the woolly mammoth.

Interested in Native American culture? Stop by the Sisseton-Wahpeton Sioux Wacipi!

Present-day South Dakota was part of France's vast Louisiana Territory. France sold this land to the United States in 1803. This was called the Louisiana Purchase.

The Sisseton-Wahpeton Sioux Wacipi

Watch the dancers and hear **traditional** songs. Meet the Sioux people and sample their foods. It's the Sisseton-Wahpeton Sioux Wacipi! (*Wacipi* is the Sioux word for "powwow.") It's held in Agency Village, south of Sisseton.

Several bands of Sioux live in South Dakota. They call themselves the Dakota, Lakota, and Nakota. The Sioux arrived from Minnesota in the 1700s. They hunted buffalo across the plains. The Black Hills were holy grounds for them.

France claimed this territory in 1682. The United States bought it in 1803. Soon many fur traders entered the region.

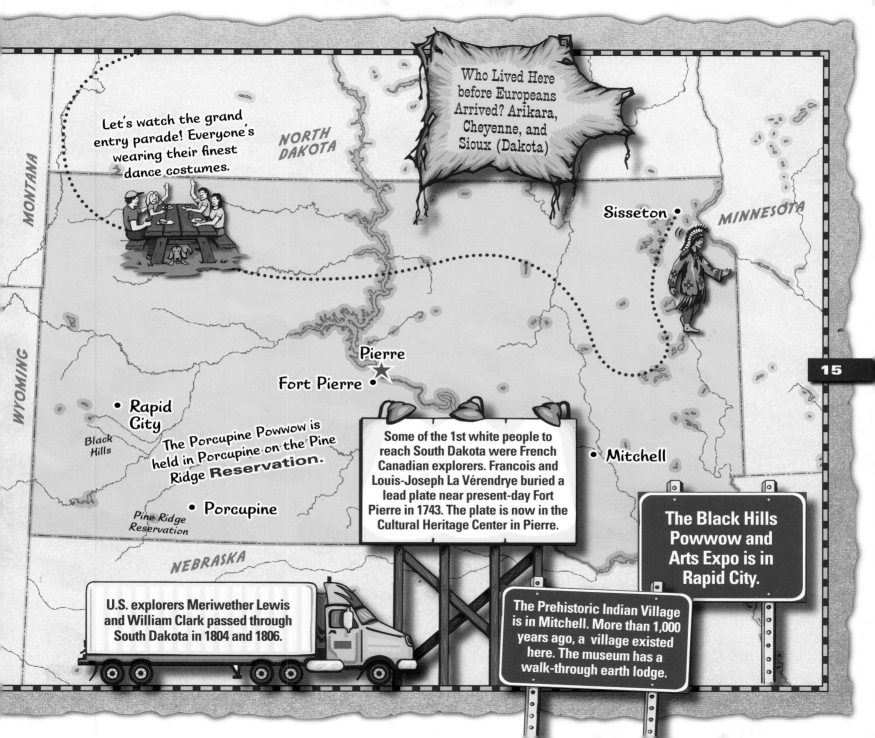

Let's watch the grand entry parade! Everyone's wearing their finest dance costumes.

NORTH DAKOTA

MONTANA

Who Lived Here before Europeans Arrived? Arikara, Cheyenne, and Sioux (Dakota)

Sisseton

MINNESOTA

Pierre

Fort Pierre

Rapid City

Black Hills

The Porcupine Powwow is held in Porcupine on the Pine Ridge Reservation.

Some of the 1st white people to reach South Dakota were French Canadian explorers. Francois and Louis-Joseph La Vérendrye buried a lead plate near present-day Fort Pierre in 1743. The plate is now in the Cultural Heritage Center in Pierre.

Mitchell

Porcupine

Pine Ridge Reservation

WYOMING

The Black Hills Powwow and Arts Expo is in Rapid City.

NEBRASKA

U.S. explorers Meriwether Lewis and William Clark passed through South Dakota in 1804 and 1806.

The Prehistoric Indian Village is in Mitchell. More than 1,000 years ago, a village existed here. The museum has a walk-through earth lodge.

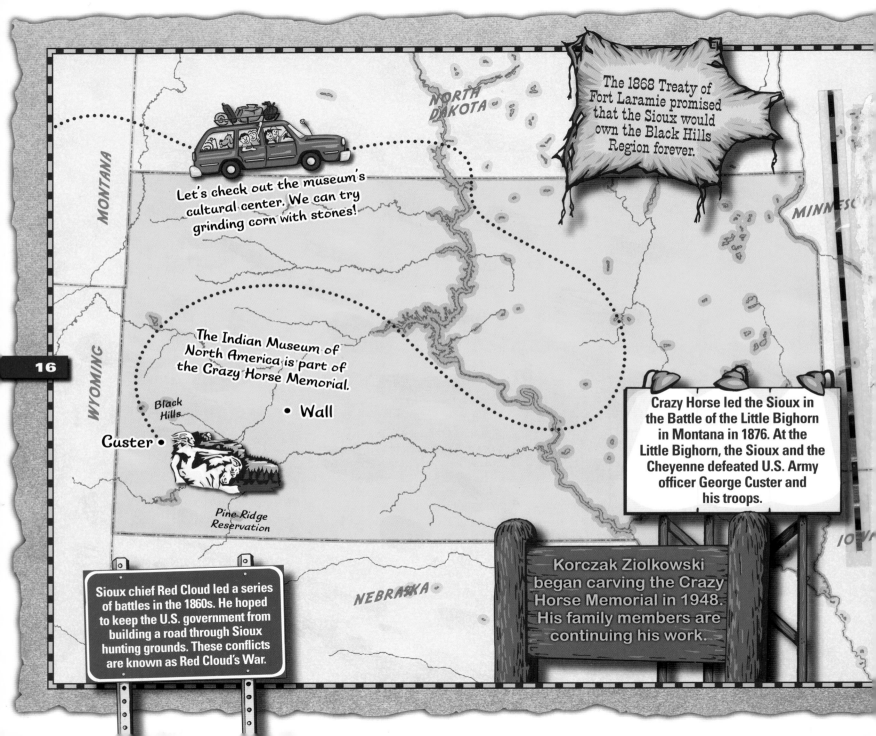

The 1868 Treaty of Fort Laramie promised that the Sioux would own the Black Hills Region forever.

Let's check out the museum's cultural center. We can try grinding corn with stones!

The Indian Museum of North America is part of the Crazy Horse Memorial.

Crazy Horse led the Sioux in the Battle of the Little Bighorn in Montana in 1876. At the Little Bighorn, the Sioux and the Cheyenne defeated U.S. Army officer George Custer and his troops.

Korczak Ziolkowski began carving the Crazy Horse Memorial in 1948. His family members are continuing his work.

Sioux chief Red Cloud led a series of battles in the 1860s. He hoped to keep the U.S. government from building a road through Sioux hunting grounds. These conflicts are known as Red Cloud's War.

MONTANA

NORTH DAKOTA

MINNESOTA

WYOMING

Black Hills

• Wall

Custer •

Pine Ridge Reservation

NEBRASKA

IOWA

The Crazy Horse Memorial near Custer

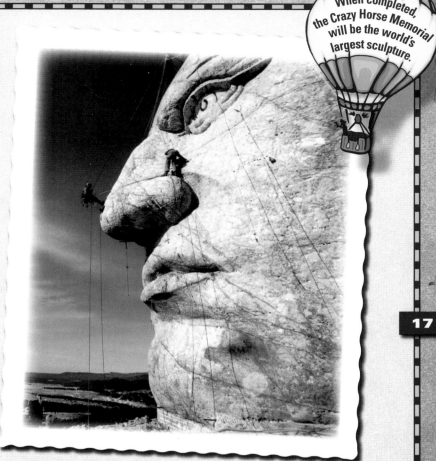

When completed, the Crazy Horse Memorial will be the world's largest sculpture.

Don't miss the Crazy Horse Memorial. It's a massive carving in a mountain. Only Crazy Horse's face has been carved so far.

Crazy Horse was a famous Sioux warrior. He and others fought to keep Sioux lands. The U.S. government met with the tribe in 1868. It promised the Black Hills to the Sioux. But soldiers entered this region in 1874. They found gold! Soon gold-seekers swarmed over the hills.

Crazy Horse and Sioux chief Sitting Bull fought bravely. But they were defeated in 1877. Later, soldiers attacked the Sioux at Wounded Knee. They killed almost 300 Sioux men, women, and children.

The Crazy Horse Memorial isn't finished yet. But check it out anyway—it's still pretty amazing!

The massacre at Wounded Knee took place on December 29, 1890. The battle site is on today's Pine Ridge Indian Reservation. The Wounded Knee Museum is in Wall.

Are we back in the 1800s? No! Deadwood features costumed actors.

Martha Jane Canary's nickname was Calamity Jane. She was an expert at horseback riding and shooting. She usually wore men's clothes.

Deadwood and the Black Hills Gold Rush

Have you heard of Wild Bill Hickok? How about Calamity Jane? They were colorful figures in the Wild West. Visit Deadwood, and you'll learn all about them. They once lived in this wild, lawless town. And they're both buried in Deadwood's cemetery.

Gold was discovered in this area in 1876. Thousands of miners rushed in. Deadwood, Custer, and Lead sprang up almost overnight. These mining towns were rough and rowdy.

In Deadwood, you'll see what life was like then. You'll visit the saloon and other old buildings. You can even tour an old gold mine!

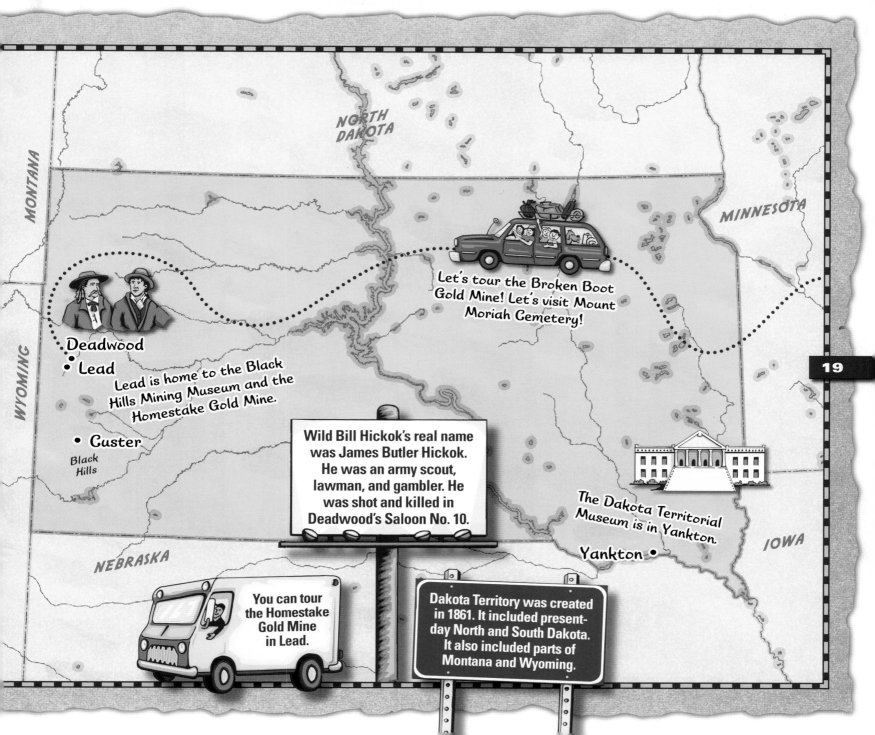

NORTH DAKOTA

MONTANA

MINNESOTA

WYOMING

Let's tour the Broken Boot Gold Mine! Let's visit Mount Moriah Cemetery!

Deadwood

Lead

Lead is home to the Black Hills Mining Museum and the Homestake Gold Mine.

Custer

Black Hills

Wild Bill Hickok's real name was James Butler Hickok. He was an army scout, lawman, and gambler. He was shot and killed in Deadwood's Saloon No. 10.

The Dakota Territorial Museum is in Yankton.

Yankton

IOWA

NEBRASKA

You can tour the Homestake Gold Mine in Lead.

Dakota Territory was created in 1861. It included present-day North and South Dakota. It also included parts of Montana and Wyoming.

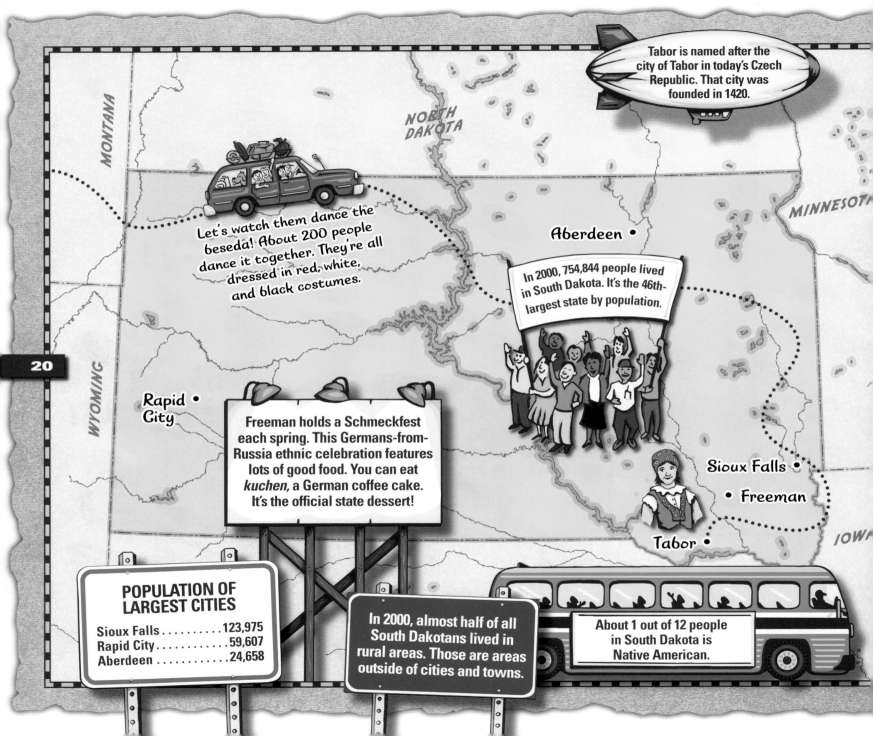

Tabor is named after the city of Tabor in today's Czech Republic. That city was founded in 1420.

Let's watch them dance the beseda! About 200 people dance it together. They're all dressed in red, white, and black costumes.

In 2000, 754,844 people lived in South Dakota. It's the 46th-largest state by population.

Freeman holds a Schmeckfest each spring. This Germans-from-Russia ethnic celebration features lots of good food. You can eat *kuchen*, a German coffee cake. It's the official state dessert!

POPULATION OF LARGEST CITIES

Sioux Falls 123,975
Rapid City 59,607
Aberdeen 24,658

In 2000, almost half of all South Dakotans lived in rural areas. Those are areas outside of cities and towns.

About 1 out of 12 people in South Dakota is Native American.

Tabor's Czech Days

Join the fun at the Czech Days parade!

Watch the folk dancers in their bright costumes. While you watch, munch on a *kolache.* It's a bun-shaped pastry with yummy filling inside. You're enjoying Czech Days in Tabor!

Czech **immigrants** began settling here in the 1860s. Their homeland was in eastern Europe. That area is now the Czech Republic and Slovakia. Tabor's Czechs love to celebrate their culture!

Many other immigrant groups settled in South Dakota. Some came from Germany, Norway, Russia, or Ireland. During the gold rush, many got mining jobs. Others worked hard to set up farms. They started new lives in this new land.

What can you fill a kolache with? Lots of things! You can use fruit, cheese, cabbage, meat, poppy seeds, or prune butter.

How did pioneers cook without electricity?
Find out at the Ingalls Homestead!

Laura Ingalls Wilder was born in Wisconsin in 1867. She was 12 when her family moved to De Smet. She died in 1957.

The Ingalls Homestead in De Smet

Have you read any books by Laura Ingalls Wilder? She wrote stories called the Little House books. Her best-known book is *Little House on the Prairie*.

Laura lived in De Smet as a girl. Several of her books take place there. One is called *Little Town on the Prairie*. And the little town is De Smet!

You can visit a farmhouse just like Laura's. It's called the Ingalls Homestead now. You can ride a horse-drawn wagon there, too. Or explore the grassy prairie. That's where Laura used to play. Imagine living there about 1880. It would have been a great adventure!

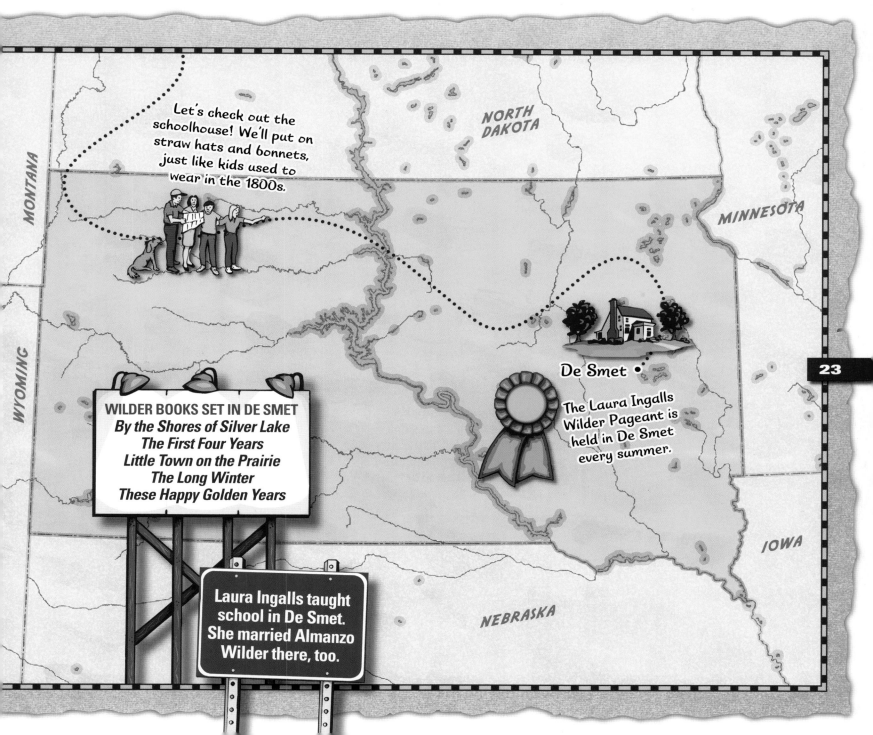

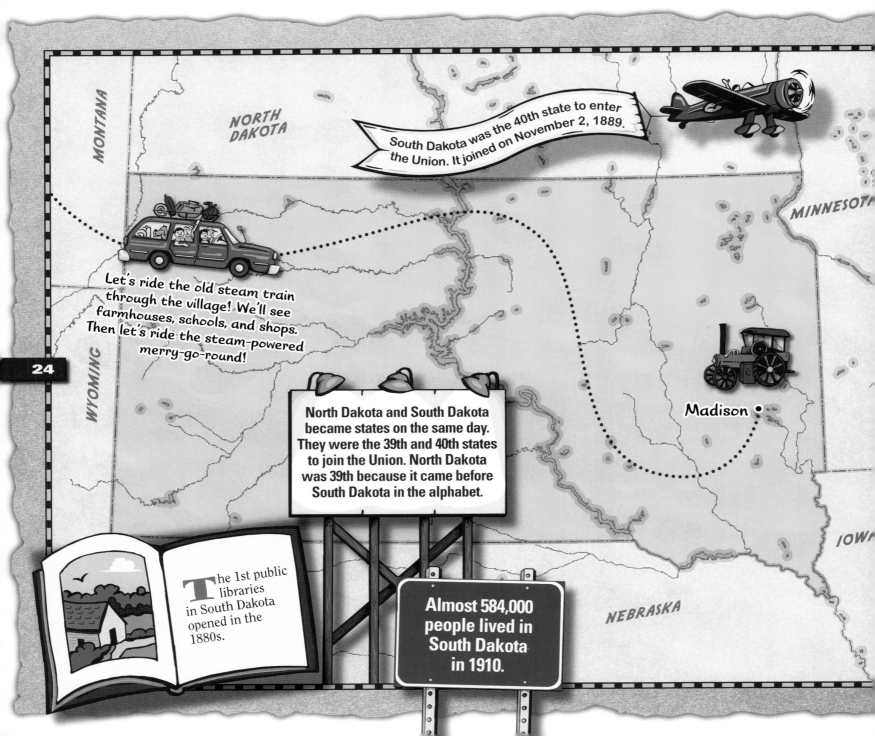

MONTANA

NORTH DAKOTA

South Dakota was the 40th state to enter the Union. It joined on November 2, 1889.

MINNESOTA

WYOMING

Let's ride the old steam train through the village! We'll see farmhouses, schools, and shops. Then let's ride the steam-powered merry-go-round!

North Dakota and South Dakota became states on the same day. They were the 39th and 40th states to join the Union. North Dakota was 39th because it came before South Dakota in the alphabet.

Madison

The 1st public libraries in South Dakota opened in the 1880s.

Almost 584,000 people lived in South Dakota in 1910.

NEBRASKA

IOWA

Madison's Prairie Village Threshing Jamboree

Old-time tractors are puffing out steam. Old farm machines are plowing away. Some are pulled by sturdy horses. It's the Prairie Village **Threshing** Jamboree!

Prairie Village is like a prairie town from about 1900. It shows how South Dakota's farmers lived then.

Gold brought many people to South Dakota. But thousands of others came to farm. They grew crops and raised cattle and other animals. Steam-powered farm machines made their work easier.

By the 1880s, railroads crossed the territory. Towns sprang up along the train routes. They were trade centers for farmers and ranchers.

Wow! South Dakota farmers worked hard in the early 1900s.

South Dakota's state motto is "Under God, the People Rule."

South Dakota lawmakers are hard at work inside the capitol.

26

Yankton was the capitol of Dakota Territory from 1861 to 1883. Then the territory's capital moved to Bismarck, North Dakota.

South Dakota once had a tiny capitol. It was just a little wooden building. Inside were state government offices. In 1910, those offices got a brand-new home. It's the magnificent capitol we see today!

South Dakota's government has three branches. One branch makes the state's laws. Its members meet in the capitol. Another branch sees that laws are carried out. The governor is the head of this branch. Judges make up the third branch. They hear cases in courts. Then they decide whether laws have been broken.

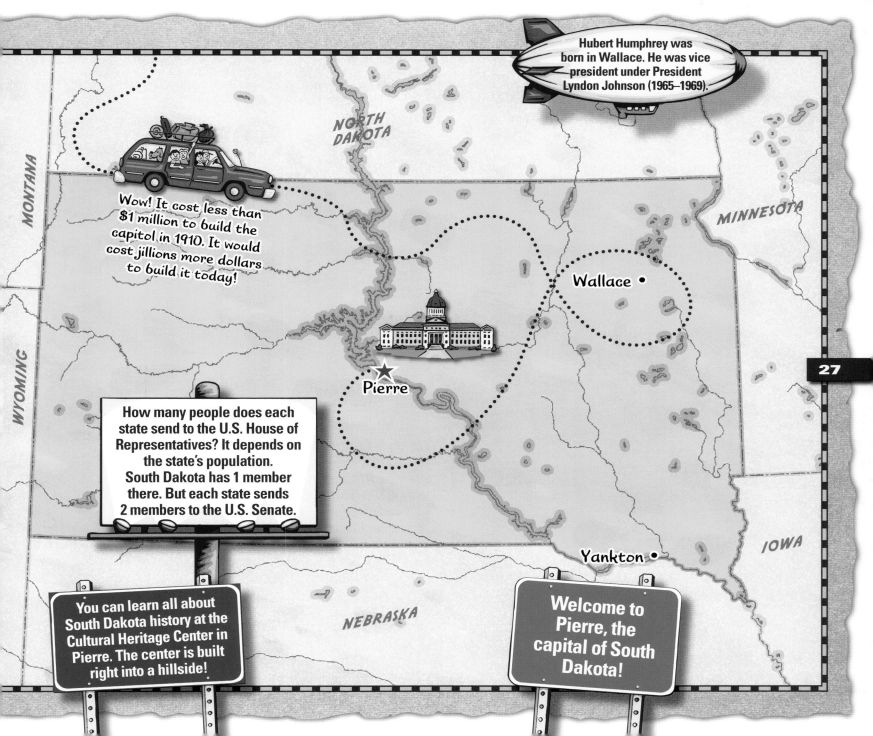

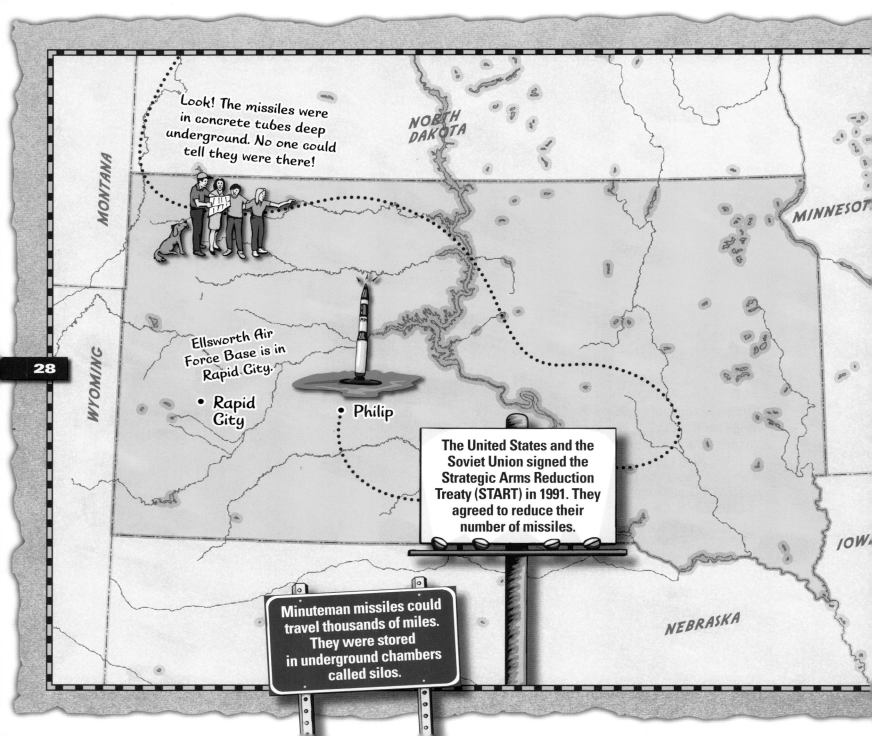

First, you visit the control center. You see walls of switches and equipment. Then you visit the launch site. A huge missile once stood ready for launch there. You're touring the Minuteman missile site!

This site was one of many built in the 1960s. The missiles were weapons for the Cold War. This war developed after World War II (1939–1945). The United States was on one side. And the Soviet Union was on the other. No war actually broke out. But both sides built weapons—just in case.

The Cold War ended in 1991. Then the Minuteman sites began closing down.

What a lot of switches! You're exploring the Minuteman missile site.

29

The Soviet Union was also called the Union of Soviet Socialist Republics (USSR). The USSR broke up into separate states in 1991.

Look closely—those pictures are made of corn! Be sure to tour the Corn Palace.

The State Agricultural Heritage Museum is at South Dakota State University in Brookings.

t looks like a big, colorful palace. Huge pictures cover its walls. But get up close. Those pictures are made of brightly colored corn!

This is the famous Corn Palace. Scenes of South Dakota life cover the walls. They're made with more than just corn. Many other grains and grasses are used, too.

South Dakotans are proud of their agriculture. That's why they built the Corn Palace!

Farms and ranches cover most of the state. Big ranches spread across western South Dakota. Most crops are grown in the east. Corn, soybeans, and wheat are the major crops.

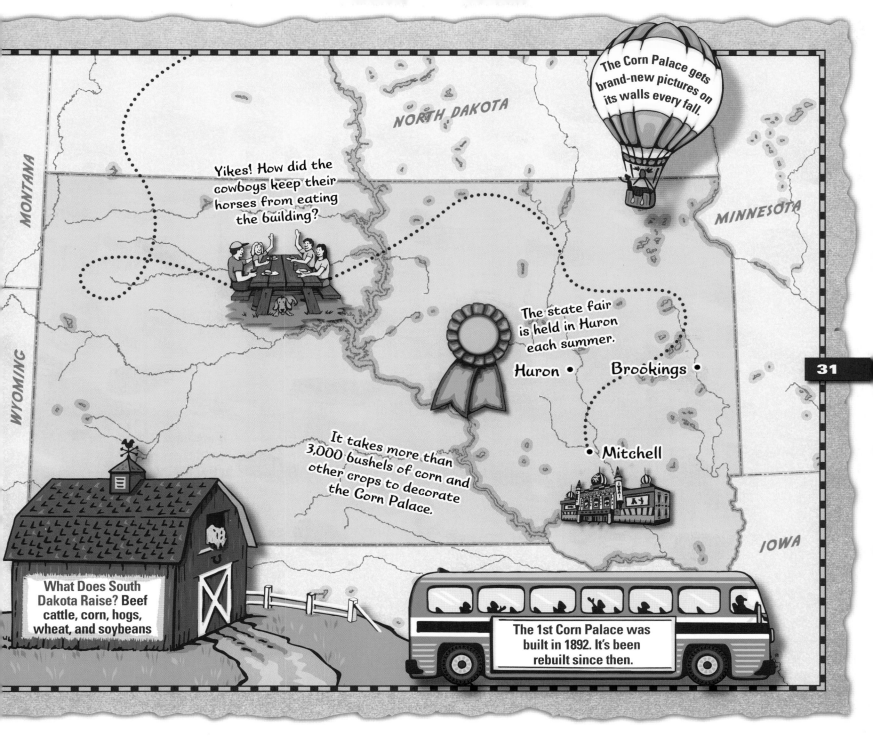

NORTH DAKOTA

MONTANA

MINNESOTA

WYOMING

The Corn Palace gets brand-new pictures on its walls every fall.

Yikes! How did the cowboys keep their horses from eating the building?

The state fair is held in Huron each summer.

Huron •

Brookings •

It takes more than 3,000 bushels of corn and other crops to decorate the Corn Palace.

• Mitchell

What Does South Dakota Raise? Beef cattle, corn, hogs, wheat, and soybeans

IOWA

The 1st Corn Palace was built in 1892. It's been rebuilt since then.

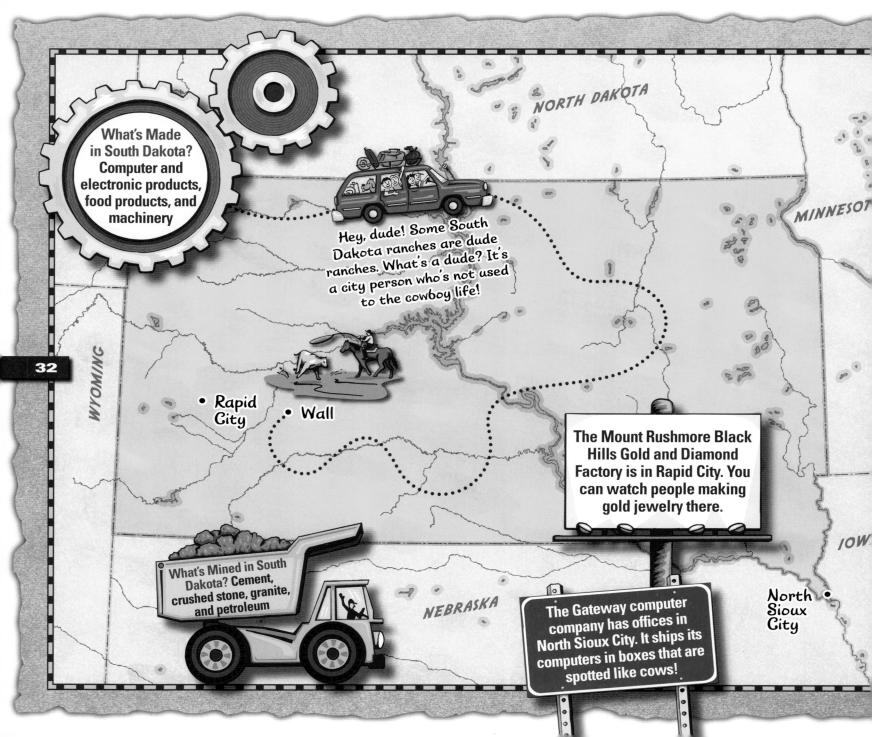

What's Made in South Dakota? Computer and electronic products, food products, and machinery

Hey, dude! Some South Dakota ranches are dude ranches. What's a dude? It's a city person who's not used to the cowboy life!

• Rapid City

• Wall

The Mount Rushmore Black Hills Gold and Diamond Factory is in Rapid City. You can watch people making gold jewelry there.

What's Mined in South Dakota? Cement, crushed stone, granite, and petroleum

The Gateway computer company has offices in North Sioux City. It ships its computers in boxes that are spotted like cows!

North Sioux City

NORTH DAKOTA

MINNESOTA

WYOMING

NEBRASKA

IOWA

Shearer's Cow Creek Ranch in Wall

R ide out on the range with the cowboys. Wear yourself out cleaning the horse stalls. Or just watch the cowboys work. You're at Shearer's Cow Creek Ranch!

This is a real cattle ranch. You can spend a whole vacation there. You can join the cowboys in their work. Or just sit back and watch.

South Dakota has thousands of cattle ranches. Beef cattle provide tons of meat. It's cut and packaged in meatpacking plants.

Meat processing is a big industry here. Some factories process milk, too. But computer equipment is the leading factory product.

Want to try out life on the range? Head to Shearer's Cow Creek Ranch!

Wall Drug Store in Wall is the world's largest drugstore. It's famous all over the world.

Fun at Lake Oahe

J ump in and make a big splash. Take a boat out and catch some fish. Or have a lakeside picnic under the trees. You're enjoying Lake Oahe!

This is South Dakota's biggest lake. It was created by Oahe Dam, near Pierre. That's a big dam on the Missouri River.

People have great fun on South Dakota's lakes. They enjoy the Black Hills and Badlands, too. Thousands of tourists visit the state every year. Some watch wildlife and take in the **scenery.** Others go to rodeos, powwows, or pioneer festivals. Historic sites are also popular. There's something for everyone in South Dakota!

Want a scenic sunset hike? Head to Lake Oahe!

The National Motorcycle Museum and Hall of Fame is in Sturgis. Motorcycles, old and new, are on display there.

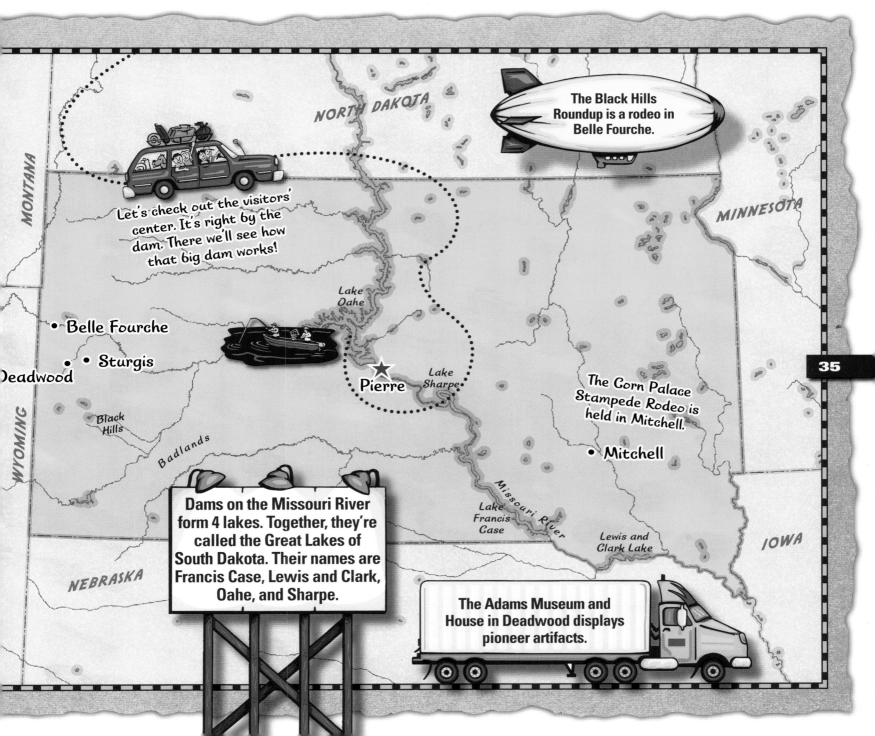

The Black Hills Roundup is a rodeo in Belle Fourche.

Let's check out the visitors' center. It's right by the dam. There we'll see how that big dam works!

The Corn Palace Stampede Rodeo is held in Mitchell.

Dams on the Missouri River form 4 lakes. Together, they're called the Great Lakes of South Dakota. Their names are Francis Case, Lewis and Clark, Oahe, and Sharpe.

The Adams Museum and House in Deadwood displays pioneer artifacts.

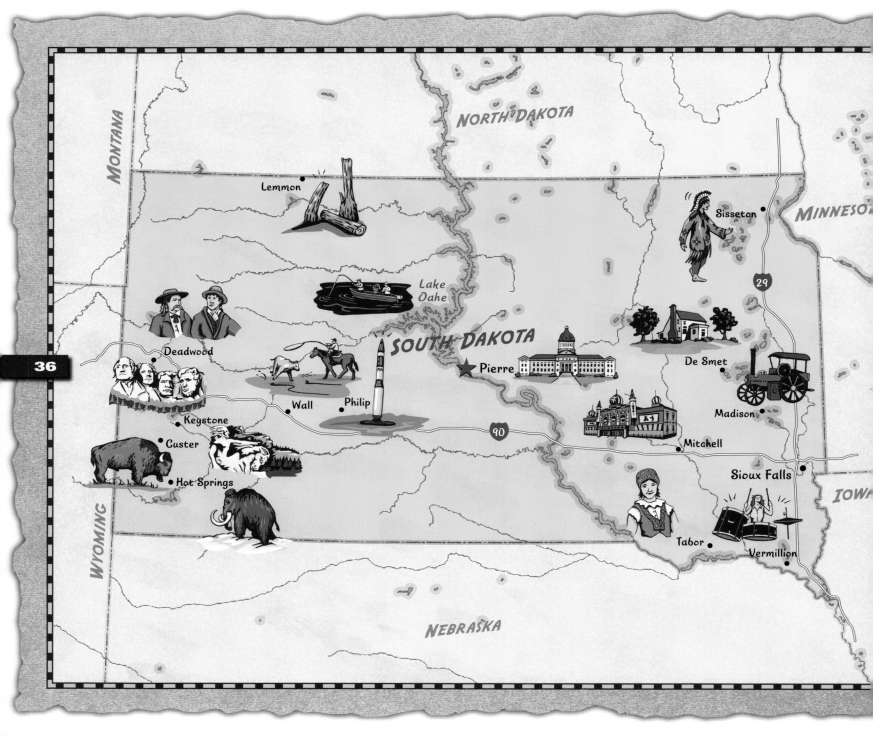

MONTANA

NORTH DAKOTA

MINNESOTA

WYOMING

NEBRASKA

IOWA

SOUTH DAKOTA

Lemmon

Sisseton

Lake Oahe

Deadwood

Pierre

De Smet

Keystone

Wall

Philip

Madison

Custer

Mitchell

Hot Springs

Sioux Falls

Tabor

Vermillion

90

29

OUR TRIP

We visited many amazing places on our trip! We also met a lot of interesting people along the way. Look at the map on the left. Use your finger to trace all the places we have been.

Who was South Dakota named for? See page 5 for the answer.

Who carved the sculptures at Mount Rushmore? Page 7 has the answer.

Where is the world's largest reptile collection? See page 8 for the answer.

When did Lewis and Clark pass through South Dakota? Look on page 15 for the answer.

What was Wild Bill Hickok's real name? Page 19 has the answer.

What is South Dakota's state motto? Turn to page 26 for the answer.

How many bushels of corn and other crops does it take to decorate the Corn Palace? Look on page 31 for the answer.

What is the world's largest drugstore? Turn to page 33 for the answer.

That was a great trip! We have traveled all over South Dakota.

There are a few places that we didn't have time for, though. Next time, we plan to visit America's Shrine to Music Museum in Vermillion. The museum has more than 10,000 musical instruments from countless cultures and historical periods. There are also live concerts and other activities.

More Places to Visit in South Dakota

WORDS TO KNOW

corrals (kuh-RALZ) holding pens for horses or other animals

fossils (FOSS-uhlz) the prints or remains of plants or animals left in stone

immigrants (IM-uh-gruhnts) people who move to another country

massacre (MASS-uh-ker) the violent killing of a large number of people

missile (MISS-uhl) a long, narrow weapon that travels a long distance

prairies (PRAIR-eez) grasslands

reservation (rez-ur-VAY-shuhn) land set aside for a special use, such as for Native Americans

scenery (SEE-nur-ee) a beautiful view of a nature area

threshing (THRESH-ing) separating grain or seeds from the stalks

traditional (truh-DISH-uhn-uhl) following long-held customs

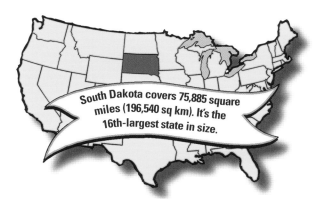

South Dakota covers 75,885 square miles (196,540 sq km). It's the 16th-largest state in size.

STATE SYMBOLS

State animal: Coyote

State bird: Chinese ring-necked pheasant

State dessert: Kuchen

State fish: Walleye

State flower: Pasque (May Day flower)

State fossil: *Triceratops*

State gemstone: Fairburn agate

State insect: Honeybee

State jewelry: Black Hills gold

State mineral: Rose quartz

State soil: Houdek soil

State tree: Black Hills spruce

State flag

State seal

STATE SONG

"Hail, South Dakota"

Words and music by DeeCort Hammitt

Hail! South Dakota, A great state of the land,
Health, wealth and beauty, That's what makes her grand;
She has her Black Hills, And mines with gold so rare,
And with her scenery, No other state can compare.

Come where the sun shines, And where life's worth your while,
You won't be here long, 'Till you'll wear a smile.
No state's so healthy, and no folk quite so true,
To South Dakota. We welcome you.

Hail! South Dakota, The state we love the best,
Land of our fathers, Builders of the west;
Home of the Badlands, and Rushmore's ageless shrine,
Black Hills and prairies, Farmland and Sunshine.
Hills, farms and prairies, Blessed with bright Sunshine.

FAMOUS PEOPLE

Anderson, Sparky (1934–), baseball manager

Barker, Bob (1923–), TV game show host

Brokaw, Tom (1940–), TV newscaster

Colvin, Shawn (1956–), singer and songwriter

Crazy Horse (ca. 1840–1877), American Indian warrior

Floren, Myron (1919–), accordionist

Goble, Paul (1933–), author

Hansen, Joseph (1923–), author

Howe, Oscar (1915–1983), artist

Humphrey, Hubert H. (1911–1978), senator and vice president (1965–1969)

Justus, Roy Braxton (1901–1983), political cartoonist

Ladd, Cheryl (1951–), actor

Lambert, Ward "Piggy" (1888–1958), basketball coach

Lawrence, Ernest (1901–1958), nuclear physicist

McGovern, George (1922–), politician

Means, Russell (1939–), American Indian activist

Provine, Dorothy (1937–), actor

Red Cloud (1822–1909), American Indian chief

Sitting Bull (ca. 1831–1890), American Indian leader

Van Brocklin, Norm (1926–1983), football player

Wilder, Laura Ingalls (1867–1957), author

TO FIND OUT MORE

At the Library

Anderson, J. Christopher. *Uniquely South Dakota*. Chicago: Heinemann Library, 2004.

Fradin, Dennis B., and Judith Bloom Fradin. *South Dakota*. Chicago: Children's Press, 1995.

McLeese, Don. *Red Cloud*. Vero Beach, Fla.: Rourke Publishing, 2004.

Yacowitz, Caryn. *South Dakota*. New York: Children's Press, 2003.

On the Web

Visit our home page for lots of links about South Dakota:
http://www.childsworld.com/links

Note to Parents, Teachers, and Librarians: We routinely verify our Web links to make sure they are safe, active sites—so encourage your readers to check them out!

Places to Visit or Contact

South Dakota Department of Tourism
Capitol Lake Plaza
711 East Wells Avenue
Pierre, SD 57501
800/732-5682
For more information about traveling in South Dakota

South Dakota State Historical Society
Cultural Heritage Center
900 Governors Drive
Pierre, SD 57501
605/773-3458
For more information about the history of South Dakota

INDEX

Bye, Mount Rushmore State.
We had a great time.
We'll come back soon!

40